30 Ways to Parent on Purpose

Changing the World Through
Intentional Parenting

JOHNATHAN HARMS

2

30 Ways
to
Parent
on
Purpose

Changing the World Through
Intentional Parenting

JOHNATHAN HARMS

TUTORDAD PRESS
www.tutordad.org

By Johnathan Harms
Published By: TutorDad Press
ISBN-10: 978-1-7328020-1-8
ISBN-13: 1-7328020-1-7

Copyright © 2018 by Johnathan Harms

tutordad.org

fb.com/johnathanharms
instagram.com/harms.johnathan

Printed in the USA

For my mighty Benaiah,

my daring Abishai,

my delightful Zibiah,

and all the other 'arrows' yet to come.

Table Of Contents

About the Author:

My name is Johnathan Harms, and I am a husband, a father, a home-educator, a blogger, and a visionary. My wife Regina and I have been best friends for 10 years and married for over eight of those years. We currently live in Northeast Texas. Regina and I are followers of Jesus and have served in the local church in various ways, including youth and deacon ministry. We've also lived and worked at an orphanage in Haiti. And more recently, we took our family on a month-long mission trip to Ghana, West Africa.

Over the years, a passion for raising the next generation has grown in us. Due to that desire, we embarked on becoming foster parents in 2014. In the last couple of years, we have been blessed with three beautiful children through adoption. We have a huge heart for intentional parenting and have big dreams for our tribe. We call it 'Parenting On Purpose'. We see intentional parenting as the number one way to truly change the world, glorify God, and minister to a broken humanity. Our desire is to bless, encourage, and inspire others in their parenting journeys.

For more articles, resources, and parenting inspiration, visit my website and blog: *tutordad.org*

Introduction

Why would a young man like me write a book about intentional parenting? My motivation to write this book has come from several different places. The number one reason why I chose to write this book is this: I see so much untapped potential in our families. *Do you see it?* God has chosen *families* to be the building blocks of our society. God wants to use your family to impact and change the world.

One of the inspirations for this book is seeing a number of fathers and mothers who have dared to live a different sort of life. They have set out to lead a life where children are prized and time together is prioritized. Their lives are lived by design. Thoughtfulness and intentionality reign in their homes. I have seen fathers and mothers who have a vision for their families that is unmarred by society's unspoken expectations. These are families that don't seek to "fit in", but rather seek to pursue God's vision and plan for them. Some are large families filled with children who love each other and have good relationships with one another. They are families that live, love, learn, and labor together. I see a generation of families rising up to change the world and make their dent in the universe. I've seen too much to settle for ordinary. Our families have so much potential!

Another motivation for writing this book is the current state of our culture. Parents, look around you. Disconnected families are the norm in the Western world. Many youths are more comfortable sharing their struggles, dreams, and desires with their peers and counselors than with their moms and dads. Often they will rather go to someone else for advice or for help. In many cases, the family is not the place of significance, the pillar of strength, or the haven of love that it is supposed to be. *Things can be different! By the grace of God and our intentional effort, we can do so much better!*

I realize that when we speak of our children and the process of raising them, I am treading on dangerous ground. These are sensitive topics. Our children are immensely precious to us. We value them and care for them deeply. This is no light matter. And that is why I want to encourage you in your parenting journey. I am working on cultivating deep, meaningful, and close relationships with my children. You probably are too. Families are the backbone of our society and our world. This world needs more solid, connected, and healthy families. Strong, successful families do not happen by accident. This will require purposeful thought and intentionality.

Lastly, I write these things because I believe that our children are priceless gifts. They are little people made in the image of God. And we have the responsibility and privilege to care for them and raise them to be *men* and *women*. As you read this book, let your vision for your family grow, and don't be afraid to dream big. The investments we make into our families are likely the greatest contributions we will make in the world. They are investments into eternity.

May this book encourage and inspire you as you change the world by being an intentional parent!

The Parenting on Purpose Pledge

"I commit to parenting with intentionality.

I will not let life just happen to my family.

I choose to recognize that God has entrusted this family to me, and I will take responsibility for my own life, and for my family-life.

I will seek God for His vision and purpose for my family.

I will dream, plan, and live according to the vision God is giving me for my family.

I will think and pray about each of my family members.

I will help my children discover their unique gifts and their specific calling in life.

I will parent on purpose."

Are you in?
#parentingonpurpose

THE HIGH CALLING OF PARENTHOOD

*

Do you ever wake up and decide that you want to change the world? Parents, you have been given exactly that calling. You are the heroes to the children in your home. You are raising, grooming, and discipling the next generation. You are changing the world each and every day that you live. *Do you understand the incredible impact you have on history through raising children?* Whenever one of your children grows in character, or reaches a milestone, the world becomes a better place, because one of its inhabitants just got better.

I believe that being a parent and raising children is the most important career in the world. Author Robert Wolgemuth speaks of the home as, 'The Most Important Place on Earth.'[1] Do you agree with that? Do you treat your home as the most important place on earth? Do we esteem our calling to be parents? Think about it, we are the mentors and trainers of the next generation.

The Urgency of Our Calling

Dads, Moms, time is escaping us...We only have our children in our homes and in our care somewhere around 18 years. Eighteen *short* years. As a parent, how does that make you feel? Does it make you want to curl up in the fetal position and cry? Or does it stir something within you?

If we want to prepare our children to be a blessing to the world, we need to do things *on purpose*. We need to put thought into what we are doing as a family. Just seeing what happens will not do.

A farmer does not simply throw seed out on a field with hopes that it will bring an abundant, healthy harvest. There is a lot of intentional preparation that goes into successful farming. Specific tools are used. The soil is tested to make sure it is healthy and balanced. The soil is carefully plowed and prepared for the seed. Then, the seeds are planted according to specific protocols, with the right density and spacing, and at the right time. Fertilizer is applied. The field is watered regularly. Herbicides are used to keep weeds at bay, and in some cases weeds are carefully done away with by hand. After all of this is done properly, there is a bountiful harvest. But it was the careful work, knowledge, diligence, foresight, and planning of the farmer that made this happen.

In the same way, we are called to a very important task. As parents, we have a high calling on our lives. We are raising the next generation. And this will require intentionality, planning, vision, foresight, diligence, patience, hard work, and persistence. Remember, we are managing the most important place on earth, our homes.

Children Are a Blessing

I believe most people have an inert desire to make a lasting impact on the world; to leave a legacy. Mankind has, at its core, a deep-seated desire for significance. Because of this hunger for meaning, we often spend much of our life seeking to find our own 'place of significance'. We need purpose.

Sadly, children are no longer viewed as a blessing in much of the Western World. Our culture sees children as a hindrance and a nuisance in many cases. Our careers, our desire for possessions, and the urge to travel or have fun has usurped our passion for our progeny. Do we not see that our children are literally a part of us? They are going to go further than we have. They will likely accomplish more than we have or can and go places we will never go. What a pride and joy to raise the next generation! The Bible says this about children:

"Behold, children are a heritage from the Lord,
the fruit of the womb a reward.
Like arrows in the hand of a warrior
are the children of one's youth.
Blessed is the man
who fills his quiver with them!"

—Psalm 127:3-5a

Do we see our kids as the priceless gifts they are? People are made in the image of God. They are precious, priceless, and ought to be prized. When children 'lose' their value in a culture, Motherhood inevitably loses its priority.

Motherhood is no longer viewed as a noble and worthwhile 'career'.

Changing the World One Life at a Time

Mothers, you are *so* important! What you do **matters!** You *are* significant. The world is counting on you to raise your little ones to be lovers of mankind and lovers of God. Society depends on *you* to guide these little ones to truth, and to teach them to appreciate what is lovely and what is good. We are counting on you to equip and prepare these children to live an effective and full life. A life that blesses the people around them.

Motherhood is a precious, powerful, and pertinent calling. Not only that, but it is often such a thankless, uncelebrated, overlooked, and under-appreciated job. Thank you, mothers, for what you do. Know that this world needs you!

✹ Captain of the Ship

Fathers, you are family heroes! You are at the helm. There is probably no one on earth that has a greater influence and sway on your children's lives than you. Your sons and daughters are looking to you as the ultimate picture of manhood. They will get many of their ideas about who God is and who *they* are from what they see in you. Your sons will look to you and think, *"That is what I want to become. That's what a man should be."* Your daughters will be prone to find a man that treats them the way you treat them and their mother. As far as your children are concerned, you are a champion and a hero. So be one! Your children are counting on you. Remember, you're the man! The buck stops with you.

Dad, you have been given the responsibility to lead your family; you chart the course, and you are the captain of the ship. I hope to inspire you to keep fighting the fight, to keep pressing in, and to purpose to lead your family well. Dads, invest deeply into your families. We have such a great opportunity to invest in something that matters, something of eternal value. There could not possibly be a better investment opportunity in all of the world than the one we have at home. Our wives, our children, our communities, and our society are all counting on us, and most importantly, our God is holding us accountable and responsible.

If God has called us to this task, Fathers, you can be sure that He has equipped us for it and will enable us to do what we are called to do. *Are we going to trust Him and take Him at His word?*

What is a Child to You?

How we see our children will affect our parenting in a huge way. Think about this question:

Is a child a blank-slate and an empty vessel to be filled, or is a child a gift from God that is to be opened and discovered?[2]

Our answer to this question will profoundly impact the way we parent our children.

#childrenareablessing

HOW TO USE THIS BOOK

✳

The ideas presented here in this book are things that Regina and I, along with others, have found helpful in our callings as parents. We are by no means perfect parents, not even close; but we are *intentional* parents. We don't want to just see what happens. We are parenting on purpose. Our purpose with this book is to inspire you on your intentional parenting journey.

Dear parent: It is advisable that you go through this book with an empty journal or notebook in hand. You can take notes and write down ideas on how to implement the things you want to do. After that, you can plan for each of these things specifically in order to take action. Hopefully this will inspire you to come up with even more of your own ideas on how to parent on purpose.

Endless reading does us little good if we do not *implement*. In this book, you may find some ideas that you will like and be attracted to. Some of the ideas may challenge you. You might even find some that you do not particularly care for. In any case, I believe you will gain a greater clarity on how *you* want to do things for *your* family. Not all of these ideas are going to be immediately relevant to you and your family. Each of our families are special and different. We have unique children with particular gifts and callings.

While none of these ideas will guarantee a perfect family-life, I will tell you that we have found them tremendously impactful in our calling as parents.

Some Premises That Undergird This Book:

- Children are a gift from God. They are not burdens. They have the capacity to make the world a better place.
- Parents have the God-given privilege and responsibility to raise their own children.
- Parents *are* experts when it comes to their children.
- Parents have a profound and exceptional impact on their children.
- There is such a thing as *'parenting on purpose'*. This means, if we are not careful, we can parent unintentionally as well.
- Parents can plan their own family life and chart their own course, according to their own vision for life. You do not have to submit to somebody else's expectations for your family. *You* are responsible for *your own* family.
- Each child is given specific God-given gifts and abilities in order to fulfill a special work or calling in their lives.

- Families are the building-blocks of society. Strong, healthy families mean solid, sound communities, churches, and societies.
- Parents are world-changers.

#1

Have regular date night!

✳

Yes! When it comes to parenting, put your marriage first. You can parent on purpose by giving your marriage priority. Your marriage is the foundation to your family. If it is weak, your parenting and family life will suffer along with it. We need a strong foundation to build on. But we know that this will require planning and intentionality.

Your children deserve to see you and your spouse cherish each other and prioritize your relationship with one another. Once you have children in the home, it is easy to become very child-centered in your family life. Realize this; you and your spouse existed as a couple before there were any children. *Your marriage comes before your children, because your marriage is the foundation to your family life.* If the marriage is weak, the family life will be lacking as well.

Ask just about any child what is most important to them, and they will tell you, "We want to know that Mom and Dad love each other." Seeing Mom and Dad love each other gives the children a great sense of safety, stability, and security. When the kids see that you take time to be together, it communicates to them that you love each other and that your marriage is important. Let's not skimp here. Your children won't be as convinced of your love for them if you don't love your spouse well. Children that grow up in a home where Mom and Dad love each other and prioritize their relationship with one another will learn a great deal about proper relationships. You know what they say, "more is caught than taught."

So love your spouse well! Your marriage will be blessed by it and your children will be grateful for it.

I want to share a special word with you single parents out there: Bravo! I'm so proud of you! You are intentionally leading your family. I know it must be hard. Keep going! Don't allow discouragement to set in. You are doing important work. In a lot of ways, you are basically fulfilling two different roles. I hope that you have a strong community and support system behind you. Stand strong.

#2

Have a weekly family meeting where you discuss how your last week went and plan for the next week.

✳

Consistent communication can do volumes in our marriages and our family life. Sit down and discuss how things are going, and where things are going from here. You can have everyone share what went well for them in the past week, and where they feel that they could improve. Talk about the highlights, and share wins and losses. What are they going to do to fix or remedy the losses? Ask everyone what they learned this week. How are you going to make next week even better?

If successful businesses and organizations do this regularly and it is important to them, shouldn't family-life be important enough to do the same? Your family is important. Remember, it is the most important place on earth. Society consists of families. You cannot have a strong society without strong communities. You cannot have strong communities without strong families. Let's be intentional with our families. You are training up the world's next leaders. Tomorrow's mothers, future fathers, the next generation of workers, are coming out of your home. Your kids will be the next entrepreneurs, missionaries, pastors, and artists that will shape the world in the coming years.

Having a regular meeting with your family will help you fathers lead your family well. It will allow everyone a chance to get on the same page, and unify behind a common vision.

It can be helpful to have some sort of framework or agenda for the meeting to guide you through these meetings. Regina and I have come up with our own 'family-planner sheet' that helps us conduct these meetings fluidly and effectively. Experiment and find out what works for you and your family. You should probably be able to finish these meetings in thirty minutes or less.

Your family is your team. So be a team. Be unified. You're all in this *together*. You win *together* and you lose *together*.

#3

Spend deliberate time observing your children and journal about your observations.

✸

In our fast-paced and distraction-filled world, it is easy to be busy and forget to spend time just watching your children. Too often we can get in front of the TV or some other screen, and fail to pay attention to our children. They grow up so fast! Eighteen years come and go just like that. Are we recognizing what God is doing in our children? Are we recognizing what He put within them? Do we see the gifts, the strengths, the challenges, and the uniqueness of each of our children?

Spend time just observing your children. Pay attention to all of the special things you notice about each child. Notice what they are interested in. What do they gravitate to?

What do you find them doing the most? What activities do they enjoy more than others? What situations seem to challenge them most? What do they seem to value? Take special note of the things you hear from them, the things you see in them, experiences you had with them, milestones they achieve, etc. Take time to write these things down in a special journal. You may want to give this journal to your child when they enter adulthood. It may be meaningful to review this journal on birthdays as a special tradition.

Then, form a habit of comparing and contrasting notes with your spouse. Share something about each child. Maybe you recall one of their cute sayings. Or a funny moment involving them comes to mind. Relate any concerns you might have for your children. This then affords you an opportunity to thank God for the good things and bring your concerns before Him together as a couple. You will probably want to write these things down; that way you can look back later and see how God answers prayers.

As we begin to pay more attention, we will start to notice more things that never stuck out to us before. We will likely begin to better understand what God is preparing our children for. We can appreciate their strengths and their interests. Their purpose and their unique life-calling may also become more apparent to us. This knowledge can in turn help us equip them for their specific calling. *In the short time we have with them, will they know and understand what God is calling them to, what their true calling and purpose in life is? Will they be confident in their strengths and abilities?* It is up to us to do all we can to ensure that they will be ready, and there is so much we can do to help them.

#4

Intentionally choose and build your community.

✸

We are all part of some sort of community. My definition of *community*, as I am using it here, is:

"A network or supporting group of like-minded people who share the same values as you do."

The people who you associate and fellowship with regularly become your community. Your community can be life-giving and encouraging, or it can be draining and dampening.

What we are talking about here is deliberately *forming* a network of people for the mutual growth and enrichment of our families. It means *choosing* our friends, our closest acquaintances, the people we spend the most time with. Our community can form by default if we allow it to. It's important that we have a network of people that are authorized to speak words of life and truth into our lives, hold us accountable, and help us bear our burdens. These are relationships that we invest in deeply. No room for superficiality here!

There is a significant difference between ministry, or "reaching out" to others, and our community that we let into our "inner-circle". Many of us would probably reach out to a drug addict, but most of us would never let them babysit our kids. Out of proper concern for our families, we don't let certain people into our "inner-circle". I realize that sometimes things are not as cut-and-dry. This can be challenging if we send our children to school. They will largely choose their own community, and there is not much we can do about that. But, we *can* choose who we spend time with collectively and who has access to our home.

Make your home a *sanctuary*. We may *reach out* and minister to others outside of the home, but our home should be a *safe haven*. And for it to be a sanctuary, we must take measures to guard it and keep it a safe place. When children are together, it is best to have some adult supervision. If this is not always possible, at least have the children play in a place that is not private or closed off. You will find some additional input on this on #12, about sexual boundaries.

Building community takes work. It also requires vulnerability; letting others into our lives. We will need to be hospitable to one another and open our hearts and our homes. It is well worth it though! Deep relationships are one of the greatest needs of mankind, and yet we often find ourselves running away from that very thing. God did not design us to live life alone. We, along with our families, have a *need* for community. Remember, if we are not intentional and proactive here, our children will likely form their own community without us.

Who do you spend the most time with? Who are your children spending the most time with?

"You are the average of the five people you spend the most time with.³"

—Jim Rohn

"Whoever walks with the wise becomes wise, but the companion of fools will suffer harm."

—Proverbs 13:20

#5

Actively read books about family-life and child-raising together with your spouse.

✴

If you're reading this book, this is likely something you are already doing. It is always helpful to have a time-frame and a plan for our activities. An idea would be to decide to read one book about family-life, child-raising, or education with your spouse every month. Now I realize that this may seem a bit extreme; But think about it, you only have approximately 18 years with your kiddos. *It's only 18 years.* Let's do all we can to parent on purpose and make a positive and lasting impact on our kids.

We will easily spend time reading books on personal-development in order to grow personally in our careers and be effective in life. Why would we not do the same with our families? Have we thought of being a parent as a career and a calling? If we do, we will be sure to develop ourselves in it. Keep reading, keep learning, keep growing! Tap into the resources that are available to you. Your children deserve you being at the top of your parenting game.

For book recommendations and resources, visit our website: http://tutordad.org/resources-for-parenting/

#6

Take individual Mommy or Daddy time with *each* of your children.

✵

When there are multiple children in the home, it can be a challenge to actually treat the children as individuals. Many times when boys or girls are close to the same age in a family they are referred to as 'the boys', or 'the girls'. Children want to be acknowledged as individuals. Taking special time with each child takes determination and intentionality.

By taking individual time with each of your kids, you are actually *tutoring* them, even if they go to school. Relationship is one of the greatest needs that a human being has. Spend time getting to know them and being there for them. You will begin to notice things about them that you may not have recognized before. See what you can discover about your children. What makes them unique? What's special about each one? How do they learn? What makes them feel loved? They will feel cherished and important if you take the time out of your busy schedule to be with them one-on-one.

Also, refer to #21, regarding love languages. This can be helpful in planning how to spend your time with your individual children.

#7

Learn something new together!

✳

Contrary to popular belief, children actually *do* want to learn. Dr. Glenn Doman, who has studied child development for decades, says this about young children in particular:

"There has never been, in the history of man, an adult scientist that has been half so curious as is any child between the ages of eighteen months and four years.
We adults have mistaken this superb curiosity about everything as a lack of ability to concentrate.[4]*"*

—Glenn Doman

There are few things that can grow a deep bond between people like learning something *together*. *So why not plan to have this wonderful experience with your children?* Determine to learn something new together regularly. Find out what interests your child, if you don't know already, and set out to learn more about it. Give your education context! In other words, make the learning relevant to your child's unique life. Put your education into the framework of real life.

Get into the habit of learning about the world around you together with your children. When you discover something new, i.e. during a nature walk, research it together when you get back home.

You may decide to take up archery, or fishing, or gardening. Maybe your child is interested in animals so you decide to raise a dog, or chickens, or rabbits. *They* will be thrilled that you are taking note of what they are interested in and that you are taking time for them. And *you* will have fun with them. Also, when children are truly interested in what they are doing, they will learn quickly and easily.

Whatever you decide to do, make it fun! Maybe you can learn about a different country by going to an authentic restaurant that serves that countries cuisine. Many times the people working there are actually *from* that country.

Ask them questions about their homeland. They will be honored and you will learn from them. Win win! There are so many fun ways to learn. Be creative and see what you can come up with.

See **#19** about *determining your family's scope and sequence* for more on this topic.

#8

Have meals together as much as possible.

✵

In our world of disconnectedness, even something as simple as having meals together can be a challenge. Plan and sacrifice for it. Make that appointment and keep it. Mealtimes at the family table are such good times for conversation, fellowship, and thanksgiving. Studies have shown that eating around the table together as a family, without phones and distractions, can be one of the best ways to keep a family connected. For some of us, this is one of the few 'free' times we have. Let's make the most of it by spending it with those we love.

Recently, an Australian company shot a video where couples were asked who they would have dinner with if they could choose anyone, living or dead. The couples cited various celebrity names, debating over who they would choose. Afterwards, the children of those couples are brought in for their own interview. They are asked the same question: *"Who would you choose to have dinner with if you could choose anybody in the world, living or dead?"* Their answer was, "Probably Mom and Dad." Some asked whether it had to be a celebrity, and said they would rather choose their whole family.

So, in their words, "Let's make time for the people who matter most." [5]

#9

Do a 'values assessment' with your family.

✵

What are your core values as a family? This exercise can help determine what each person's (those old enough) top ten are, and then narrow it down to top three. Then you can see how each person's values intersect collectively.

Here is a list of common values to get you started:

Abundance	Agility	Boldness
Acceptance	Ambition	Bravery
Action	Appreciation	Brilliance
Accountability	Availability	Calmness
Achievement	Authenticity	Candor
Adaptability	Balance	Capability
Adventure	Beauty	Caring
Affection	Benevolence	Challenge

Cheerfulness	Fidelity	Intensity
Cleanliness	Fitness	Intimacy
Collaboration	Flexibility	Intuitiveness
Commitment	Fluency	Investment
Confidence	Focus	Joy
Creativity	Forgiveness	Justice
Credibility	Fortitude	Kindness
Curiosity	Freedom	Knowledge
Daring	Friendship	Leadership
Dedication	Frugality	Learning
Dependability	Fun	Liberty
Determination	Genuineness	Logic
Devotion	Giving	Love
Dignity	Goodness	Loyalty
Diligence	Grace	Mastery
Discipline	Gratitude	Maturity
Discovery	Growth	Meaning
Discretion	Happiness	Merit
Diversity	Harmony	Mindfulness
Duty	Hard Work	Modesty
Education	Health	Money
Eagerness	Helpfulness	Motivation
Effectiveness	Heroism	Natural
Efficiency	Holiness	Neatness
Elegance	Honesty	Nonconformity
Empathy	Honor	Nonviolence
Encouragement	Hopefulness	Openness
Endurance	Hospitality	Opportunity
Energy	Humility	Optimism
Enjoyment	Humor	Order
Enthusiasm	Intentionality	Orderliness
Eternity	Imagination	Organization
Exploration	Independence	Originality
Expressiveness	Influence	Outlandishness
Extroversion	Ingenuity	Passion
Fairness	Initiative	Peace
Faith	Innovation	Perfection
Faithfulness	Inspiration	Persuasiveness
Family	Integrity	Perseverance
Fearlessness	Intelligence	Persistence

Personal Growth	Proactivity	Reason
Philanthropy	Progress	Recognition
Pleasure	Prosperity	Reflection
Poise	Prudence	Regularity
Positivity	Punctuality	Relationships
Power	Purpose	Reliability
Practicality	Quality	Religion
Preparedness	Quiet	Resilience
Presence	Rationality	Resourcefulness
Preservation	Realism	Respect
Responsibility	Skill	Timelessness
Righteousness	Solidarity	Tradition
Rigor	Speed	Tranquility
Restraint	Spirit	Trust
Romance	Spirituality	Truth
Sacrifice	Spontaneity	Understanding
Safety	Stability	Uniqueness
Security	Status	Unity
Selflessness	Stewardship	Valor
Self-Control	Strength	Variety
Self-Discipline	Success	Vigor
Self-Reliance	Support	Vision
Seriousness	Sympathy	Well-being
Sensitivity	Synergy	Wisdom
Serving	Teamwork	Wonder
Sharing	Thrift	Zeal
Simplicity	Thoroughness	
Sincerity	Timeliness	

What do each of you (that are old enough) value? Is there considerable overlap among all of you? Discuss: How do you determine what has the most value for you personally and as a family? How do these values change and shape your family-life? Are these values upheld in your family culture, conduct, and daily life? Are we living according to our professed values? This can be quite an eye-opening experience.

#10

Dream together, set goals to move towards those dreams, and form habits to accomplish those goals.

✳

This item is a three step process. *Dream* daringly, *plan* bold goals, and then *form* habits that get you moving in the direction you want to go.

Let's start with dreaming up a vision for our families:

First, dream big:

If you could do anything as a family, what would you do? Where are you guys headed? What is your vision for life?

It's all too easy to let dreams die. 'Reality' seems to unravel our dreams and pull us back out of the clouds all too often. But, if we don't dream, we won't reach higher. Where there is no vision, there is nothing to aspire to (Proverbs 29:18). If we don't think of what could be, we will be complacent or content with what is. Steven Covey, in his book *'The 7 Habits of Highly Effective People'*, makes the case that all things are created twice. *"There is first a mental creation, in our minds, and then a physical creation."*[6] Our actions are born out of our thoughts. Dreams are thoughts. So dream big for your family! Don't settle for the ordinary for laziness' sake. Parent, God put you in this time-space and gave you a family that you are to lead. There is so much potential to bless the world through your family!

Any dream that is worth chasing will push us to grow. Our aspirations should lead us slightly out of our comfort zone. If your dreams don't inspire you, you've aimed too low. *Is there such a thing as an average or mediocre dream?* A vision, by its very nature, is something to be reached for. It is something that is beyond average. It should be something that seems somewhat unrealistic, but reasonable enough that one might actually dare to go for it. Imagine something so grand that it puts a fire in your soul and makes your heart leap. Friend, aim for an extraordinary life! You only have one life, so you might as well make it exceptional, right?

It could be that God has put a certain desire in your heart, and maybe that desire is tied to a particular work or calling that He has prepared for you. But sometimes we are too busy, distracted, or afraid to take action. We can draw near to God's heart and pay attention to what He is feeling, and what He is looking at in this world.

"If you are not willing to risk the usual, you will have to settle for the ordinary."[7]

—Jim Rohn

"Dream no small dreams for they have no power to move the hearts of men."[8]

—Johann Wolfgang von Goethe

Where there is no vision, there is nothing to hope for. Don't let that be your family. Dream together, and form a vision for your family, then go and live it out!

Next, map out 3 yearly goals as a family.

Now that you have dreamed big, what goals do you need to set as a family to support these dreams? We don't want mediocre goals, we want goals that move us in the direction of our dreams. And if we don't know where we are going, how do we know when we get there? In light of your dreams, what goals do you need to set in order to make your vision a reality? What do you as a family want to accomplish?

Plan three yearly goals that will help you make your family dreams a reality. It's amazing that so few people make a habit of establishing goals in their lives. There's a saying that goes, "If you aim for nothing, you will hit it every time." This rings true in all areas of life, including our family-life. So set the bar high, and begin to take aim at what you, as a family, desire to accomplish in life. There is no guarantee that you will absolutely accomplish every goal you set. But, if you pursue goals, you *will* be moving forward in life, that is for certain.

It may be helpful and special to take a weekend or a night out with your spouse to think about and plan for these sorts of things. Spending some time away from our normal surroundings can help us see outside the box and gain a greater clarity in our planning. Too often we are so preoccupied with the here-and-now and all the things we need to do. The dishes in the sink, the laundry needing to be folded, the garage needing to be cleaned out, the grass needing mowing, etc. Getting away from time to time seems to spark in us a special creativity and help us gain a greater vision for what could be.

This is a big deal! You are charting the course for your 'family-ship'. This is exciting, inspiring, invigorating stuff! Yes! I know you are going places, and now you know where you are going too.

Finally, form habits that will allow you to achieve your goals:

What are some habits that can help you achieve these goals and move in the direction of your dreams?

Do you run according to a set schedule at home? Or is there just an established routine that has found its way into your home by default? I know many times we can get into a rut, and things begin to just happen in our homes. We stay up late, and thus we sleep late. Then we begin to get behind. We start compromising and sacrificing where we can't afford to. Remember, we all have habits. Sometimes we develop habits unintentionally. We cannot afford to be careless or apathetic here.

Success-mentor Darren Hardy says this about habits and success:

"Since your outcomes are all a result of your moment-to-moment choices, you have incredible power to change your life by changing those choices. Step by step, day by day, your choices will shape your actions until they become habits, where practice makes them permanent. Losing is a habit. So is winning." [9]

Our habits shape our behavior, and our behavior determines to a large degree the course and direction of our lives. Never underestimate the power of habit. In a very real sense we are what we habitually do. Writers become writers because they *write*. Leaders become leaders because they *lead*.

The joy and hope in this is that we have the power and opportunity to be *proactive* here. Let's begin to think deliberately about our habits, and which ones need to go, and which ones we need to create. *What habits can you establish as a family that will support your values, goals, and ultimately, your dreams?*

Don't lose hope or feel defeated if you fail to accomplish one of your goals, or if you have to change your goals because an unexpected situation comes up. Sometimes we have to make adjustments. Things may turn out differently than we had expected. Some of the goals that Regina and I have set we have had to later postpone. Other things we thought were far in the future have been attainable sooner than we expected. Be expectant! Press on and keep moving! Be a family that has a godly vision for life.

#11

Give your children a right view of sexuality.

✳

In the beginning, God created male and female. He differentiated and separated the two. We call this state of differentiation *sexuality*. Sexuality is a beautiful, God-created aspect of our lives as humans. At first, man was alone, but God created a suitable partner for him, the woman. The two would complement each other. The one would have certain strengths, and the other would have different strengths. The one would have certain special qualities, and the other also. Their anatomy would differ in some ways. Women were gifted to conceive and bear children, men cannot. The man contributes semen, the woman contributes the egg. God then told the man and his wife to be fruitful and multiply. So then, the two became one, and children came about as a result of the sexual union of Adam and Eve.

Sexuality, however, has been under assault for ages. It is continually perverted and twisted into something it is not. God created sex and sexuality. He made male and female. And, not surprisingly, they are *different. Are we teaching the children about these differences?* Now, the most obvious differences are anatomical. Males have beards, penises, and testicles. Females have ovaries, vaginas, and breasts that produce milk to nourish their offspring.

There are also the masculine and feminine differences in persona and character. Masculinity generally is more focused on truth, firmness, correction, courage, willingness to fight, etc. Femininity is stronger on love, nurturing, compassion, and tenderness. These are general statements, and there are many women and men that are strong in both types of qualities.

This can also lead into teaching on the sacred beauty of marriage and sexual intimacy. Do your children know that sex, in the context of marriage, is sacred and blessed by God? Do they know that they can talk to you and ask you questions about anything, even sex?

Where is your child getting his or her view of sexuality from? Culture? Movies? Pornography? Peers? Are you the source of your child's knowledge and view of sexuality or will your children seek to be informed from someone or something else?

We live in a world where pornography, casual fornication, and marital unfaithfulness are all becoming increasingly common. In light of our troubles as a society, we have a marvelous opportunity to protect our children and change the course of their lives. By speaking to our children truthfully and forthrightly about sexuality we can help them develop a godly view of sex.

"You might think that sex would be a sensitive and even an embarrassing subject for children...so they would naturally be more comfortable learning about it from people other than their parents. But not so.
The Kaiser Foundation reports that medical research and public health data tell us that when young children want information, advice, and guidance, they turn to their parents first." [10]

—Josh McDowell

For more resources on this, see our resource section online at: https://tutordad.org/resources-for-parenting/

#12

Help your children develop proper sexual boundaries.

✴

Statistics show that 1 in 10 children experience sexual abuse before the age of eighteen. For girls alone, the number is 1 in 7.[11] What a terrible tragedy! As parents, we all desire to keep our children as safe as we reasonably can. We cannot put them in a bubble, but we can take measures to help keep them from unnecessary harm. Parents can be proactive without being paranoid. One way we can protect our children is to help them develop sexual *boundaries.*

A very significant way we can protect our children sexually is to properly educate them about their body parts. Make a habit out of calling their 'private parts' by their real names. "That is your penis, son. Nobody is allowed to touch your penis." That way, should someone ever try to touch their private parts, our children will be able to tell us what happened with clarity. We can then take preemptive action, because we are aware of what is going on. *Sexual abusers are protected when people stay silent.* Let's teach our children to be aware and to always confront inappropriate behavior. Let's train them to yell and tell.

Here is a slightly humorous example of the effectiveness of this sort of instruction: Once, our 3 year old son was staying at grandma's house for the weekend. Grandma and him were at a park and the little guy needed to urinate urgently. So, grandma had to help him quickly go so that he did not wet his pants. At this time, our son firmly reminded grandma that nobody was to touch his penis. To this, she had to help him understand that it was okay if he needed help when using the restroom. Apparently the training we have done has made an impression on him. He has boundaries. He is learning what behavior is appropriate and what is not.

Some ideas here are, always keep bedroom doors open when children are playing together. Some parents have even kept the bedrooms off-limits to guests, and let the children play in the living area or playroom instead. Parents can be involved, and not let children and their guests play unsupervised for extended periods of time.

There is more information from Darkness to Light on the topic of sexual abuse at: https://www.d2l.org/

#13

Put together a 'dream-board' for each of your children.

✵

A *dream-board* is a physical or digital place for your child to visually put down their dreams, goals, and aspirations.[12] Put pictures on display there that depict aspects of their dreams and interests to make it more visual. Put your child's 'dream-board' where it will be seen often. You want it to inspire your child to reach for their dreams and to remind you to help them get where they are going.

The 'dream-board' can be as simple or creative as you and your children want to make it. Let it speak to the passions, interests, and dreams that are within them. For example, maybe your young son is into tractors and machines. You can help him put pictures of tractors and farm-life on his board, even if he is too young to understand how to do it himself. Older children may opt to do something different with this idea. An older girl may rather want a special 'board' on Pinterest. Again, be creative, and make sure to be involved and enthusiastic no matter what direction you may take with this.

The bottom line is, show your children that you are interested in and excited about their lives, and that you notice and value their interests. Cheer them on in their individual strengths, passions, and interests.

#14

Create your own special family traditions.

✹

Every family has a culture, and certain traditions with it. What sort of culture do you want to build in your family? Tradition, as used here, is: *Established practices that are often tied to one's beliefs and heritage.*[13] These can vary widely, as some cultures have a strong history of firm traditions that are adhered to nigh religiously. While there may be nothing wrong with these cultural traditions, we need to be sure that we are creating the culture we desire in our families.

Talk about traditions you would like to start in your family. Consider what you value as a family. Let the values you hold guide your culture-building endeavors. We live in a time where tradition is almost despised. We want everything to be new and novel. We need to remember that there is value and blessing in heritage. Newer isn't always better. Some things are *timeless*. Traditions are a way to convey our family culture to the next generation.

Think back to the stories you heard growing up. Stories are a powerful tool to transfer culture from one generation to another. They easily stay in our minds and leave a deep impression on us. Incorporate the power of story in your family life. Tell your children your love-story. Share with them what it was like growing up in your day. For us, we even tell our children their birth and adoption stories. We want to acknowledge their life-story, which God is scripting together with us.

The ideas listed below are simply here to get you thinking about what traditions you want to create in your family.

One tradition we have started is that we end off our year with a 'Time of Reflection'. We look back on our experiences over the last year and list maybe 10 or 20 of the best things that happened that year. We can see what we accomplished and different answers to prayer, etc. We also keep a 'Thanksgiving Jar' on the counter, in which we put random notes of what we are thankful for. We review these notes as part of the 'Year-end Time of Reflection'. Also, going through journal entries from that year is helpful. We will usually have a cup of coffee and a special dessert as part of this tradition. This tradition helps us see all that God has done and what we can be thankful for. It also gives us greater direction for the year to come.

Some people celebrate the entire 'Advent' season. There is a countdown to the day of Christmas. There are verses read in a certain order, special songs played, peculiar decorations hung, etc. Our family was in Ghana, Africa during the Pentecost season this year. Great preparations were made at the mission we were staying at and the entire time was regarded with anticipation. There was a fast instigated, much time spent in prayer and praise, and ended off with a celebration. It was a very special time.

#15

Take time to *train* your little ones, not just discipline them.

✳

Of all the ideas listed here, this one is possibly one of the most impactful. Most if not all parents *discipline* their children in some way or other. But how many of us consistently *train* our young ones? It's interesting, we can train our *dogs* how to sit, wait, fetch, roll over, be quiet, and shake a paw but it is so challenging to have our children sit still and quiet in church. Or be respectful at the dinner table. I know this because we have been dealing with these issues ourselves. It can be quite tough!

Discipline, in the paternal sense, is referring to correction and consequences for wrongdoing. Training is what we do *before* there is a need to discipline. It deals with instruction and teaching. We can intentionally create situations for our young children where we can teach them and instruct them in what they should do and what they should not do. Discipline will be more effective if there is training *first*. Discipline is consequences for misbehavior, training is the guidance and instruction to help a child to behave himself appropriately in the first place.

We can avoid many of the disciplining moments by giving proper attention to training and instruction. This takes intentionality and wisdom. It is not hard to simply miss these opportunities to *train,* and wind up having to discipline later as a result. Some of this training and instruction can happen during your weekly family meetings. Good and right behavior can be acknowledged and praised, and misbehavior can be acknowledged and corrected.

*"Fathers, do not provoke your children to anger, but bring them up in the **discipline** and **instruction** of the LORD."*

—Ephesians 6:4

Some people love their children, but they don't like them very much. I realize this sounds harsh. Let's think about this though. Some people, although they would do anything for their kids, are happy and relieved at the end of the summer when they can send their children back to school. They want their children "out of their hair". Folks, it does not have to be this way. Yes, parenting is hard. And sometimes we *need* a break. I don't know about you, but I like to be around my kids. I want them with me. I cherish the moments we have together, and would rather have more time with them, not less.

If we train our children properly, we can **love** them *and* **like** them too. Properly trained children are a joy to be around. In our home, we have a focus on *fellowship*. We don't want our children yelling at the dinner table because it takes away from fellowship. We can't talk to each other if all of the kids are shouting and making a lot of noise. So, we have them speak instead of shout. If, during play, one of the children's behavior is causing another to suffer, it's not fun anymore. So we try to put a stop to that sort of behavior. We seek to *train* them to think about how their actions affect others, and to think about being kind to others.

Discuss what your children need to learn and then plan out specific ways you can implement the needed training lovingly and effectively.

For more resources on this, see:
http://tutordad.org/resources-for-parenting/

*"It has been said that the essence of teaching is causing another to **know**. It may similarly be said that the essence of training is causing another to **do**. Teaching gives knowledge. Training gives skill. Teaching fills the mind. Training shapes the habits. Teaching brings to the child that which he did not have before. Training enables a child to make use of that which is already in his possession."* [14]

—H. Clay Trumbull

"Train up a child in the way he should go; even when he is old he will not depart from it."

—Proverbs 22:6 ESV

#16

Stay active and get fit together with your kids.

✴

One of our sons is very agile and adept at pretty much anything physical. He rode his bike a week after he turned 3 without any training wheels. He climbs on stuff, does flips on the trampoline, and is altogether very able physically. Our other son is not as keen on various physical activities. Because of this, we have made special effort to "train" with our children. We seek to "train" them, even in the physical sense. We help them do pull-ups and handstands. We do flashcards intermixed with jumping jacks, squats, or push-ups. We also enrolled them in a gymnastics class for toddlers for a season.

Have a family sport, whether it is shooting hoops, snowboarding, ping-pong, hacky sack, ultimate frisbee, mountain-bike trail riding, or any other fun sport that keeps you active. Plan a nature-hike with your kids. Jump on the trampoline with them (You may want to make sure you're in suitable shape first). I don't know about you, but I want to be in shape so that I can be involved in those sort of things. I do understand how difficult this can be. Fitness has been a challenge for me lately, because, like many of you, I have worked at a desk for the past several years. *But our children deserve to have our best, right?* If at all possible, we should strive to be fit enough to participate in activities with our children. We will be healthier for it, and we can grow closer to our kiddos in the process. That's a double win if you ask me!

Some friends of ours, who have 11 children, and happen to be in their upper 40's, go skiing with their children regularly every winter season. It's a family sport, and they love it. Another family we know, which also happens to be a large family, plays ultimate frisbee together, and they are quite intense with it as well. Another father does paintballing with his sons. They get pretty into it too. They perform the missions at hand and execute their battle plans with precision. Be creative, and if you don't already have a sort of 'family-sport', find something that you all can enjoy at some level and get to it.

The bottom line is, have fun together! Team up with some other families that have similar interests and have a blast!

#17

Have regular devotional time together as a family.

※

Again, you will need to make an appointment and keep it! Prioritize your family devotional life. This will bring you guys closer together as you get to know God better. We like to switch it up sometimes. We will go through Psalms or Proverbs, and then maybe do a devotional book, and then read through a biography. Whatever you do, be consistent. It is so hard to do something if you don't do it consistently. Set a time that works with your schedule. We have found that mealtimes work best for us since we are all together anyway. The children were in highchairs when we began doing this, and we would let them eat while we read to them.

We like to read out of a book or out of the Bible, sing, and pray together, with each child taking his or her turn. Find out what works best for your family. A side-note here: Having a habit of family devotions at home will make it easier for your children to sit through Church or Bible-Study. We've noticed that when we have consistently had times of family devotions at home, church and other events have gotten easier for our children.

There are books, devotionals, study guides, and discipleship programs that have helped us navigate the seemingly murky waters of family devotions. It can be hard to know where to start, and you don't want to start something just to later on lose direction and quit.

For more ideas, help, and guidance regarding family devotions, visit: https://heroiclifediscipleship.com/

#18

Read books together as a family.

✷

Books are worlds that are just waiting to be opened. So why not open up these new worlds to your children through reading to them? This is especially beneficial for young children that do not read much yet. Extensive reading as a family will grow their vocabulary, and expand their horizons. It will broaden the scope of their knowledge and expand their worldview. Also, it will allow them to vicariously experience different adventures themselves.

Reading together as a family is an especially good activity for the winter months when spending more time inside is desirable. You can live an adventure together with your family through books. Reading is better than endless movies and videos, because it requires everyone to use their minds and their imaginations. The books you read together as a family will profoundly affect the culture of your family.

Earlier, we mentioned the power of story, and this rings true when it comes to books as well. These books you read through with your family will leave a lasting impact on the souls of your little ones. Stories make the world go round. They stick in our memories. Stories educate in a relatable and often indelible way. They leave a deep impression.

Another powerful aspect of reading to your children is narration. Basically, after reading, have each child repeat back to you, in their own words, what they heard. Older children that read can take turns reading aloud during your reading times.

"There are many little ways to enlarge your child's world. Love of books is best of all." [15]

—Jacqueline Kennedy Onassis

"A reader lives a thousand lives before he dies." [16]

—George R.R. Martin

#19

Determine your family's scope-and-sequence.

✵

What skills, knowledge, and experiences do you think your children should have? And by when do you think they should acquire it? This is essentially your family's *'scope-and-sequence'*. I think we probably all know that children don't learn *everything* they need to know about life in school. Today, many children are taught a great number of things that are not even relevant to their lives. Time is spent on things that are likely unnecessary. On the other hand, children often don't learn many of the things they need to know to be effective in life. We need to be intentionally ensuring, to the best of our ability, that our children are equipped for life.

Have meetings with your spouse where you discuss what knowledge and skills you think your children should have.

Think about the skills and knowledge you desire your children to have. List specific things so that you can plan to equip them. Then plan your family life in such a way that you can impart these things to them.

Some families I know work cattle with their children. Others have learned Hebrew and Greek with their children to help them study the Bible. A father that I know built a large greenhouse to farm tomatoes for the purpose of helping his children learn about business and work. Another family that ran a tree-servicing business bought a wood-splitter so that their ten year-old son could learn about work and business. This boy had not wanted to learn math at all, but now, after starting his own business splitting firewood, he learned quickly. *What do **you** feel your children should know? What is your vision for them?*

This will largely be determined by what you value and the vision you have for your family. If you value self-reliance and survivalism, you may want your children to learn how to grow their own crops and raise animals. You may value leveraging your time more and thus want your children to rather spend time learning highly valuable, marketable skills. Some value sports more than others...maybe you want to have a football 'training-camp' at your house and train your young men to be excellent athletes. If you prize biblical truth and the Gospel of Jesus Christ, you may want your children to be fluent in a foreign language(s) to better prepare them for the mission field. The important thing here is that you act in accordance with *your* values.

#20

Be the curator of your museum of memories.

✵

Families are really like a museum of memories. Think back into your collection of memories...What are some meaningful experiences you had as a child? There are no doubt particular experiences that remain etched in your memory. These are memorable moments from your childhood that left a lasting impact on you. Maybe it is a trip to the Grand Canyon. Some families have an annual camp-out every summer. You may have many memories of helping dad on the farm. Maybe you remember the year you lived in a travel-trailer with your mom and dad and six siblings. List some experiences that you want to give your children, and make a plan to do them.

Again, this goes hand-in-hand with what your particular vision is for your family. What do you want to accomplish, and what do you as a family value? How are you going to arrange a life full of rich memories for your family?

"A museum has a selection of things worth preserving. There are art museums, natural-history museums, maritime museums, and those preserving documents of a variety of kinds...Had someone not had the idea of selecting and putting things together in some sort of order, much of past history would be lost as far as the vividness of reality given by the collections of things in museums. What is a family meant to be? Among other things, I personally have always felt it is meant to be a museum of memories – collections of carefully preserved memories and a realization that day-by-day memories are being chosen for our museum."[17]

—Edith Schaeffer

What if we thought about it this way: *your family is a museum of memories?* And you, the parent, are the curator of that collection of experiences.

How's your museum coming along?

#21

Become acquainted with the 5 love languages and determine which one is your child's primary love language.

✳

*Do your kids **know** that you love them?* That's a strange question to ask, I know. Dr. Gary Chapman's books, 'The 5 Love Languages' and the 'The 5 Love Languages of Children' document five unique ways in which love is conveyed and received.[18]

The Five Love Languages they discovered are as follows:
- ❖ *Gifts*
- ❖ *Quality Time*
- ❖ *Physical Touch*
- ❖ *Acts Of Service*
- ❖ *Words of Affirmation*

Out of Dr. Chapman's studies, it was discovered that each individual person prefers certain love languages over others. A person's favored love language is referred to as their primary love language. Find out how to determine what your children's (and spouse's) primary love language is by reading their book. They also have a *love languages questionnaire*' you can also fill out that is available on their website, which can definitely be a helpful resource in determining how your child gives and recieves love.

By consistently expressing your love to your children in their primary love languages you will ensure that they really *know* that you love them.

For further insight into this topic, see Dr. Chapman's book, *The Five Love Languages of Children: The Secret to Loving Children Effectively.* His book is a phenomenal and crucial help for anyone who wants to parent intentionally.

#22

Allow your children to help you. Have your children do chores and meaningful work to help out wherever they can.

✳

Plan and map out what needs to be done in the family and divide up the responsibilities accordingly and appropriately. Find ways for your young ones to participate in what you are doing. Let them be relevant and needed in your family.

One thing might be mowing the lawn. I have often had one of my toddlers 'help' me mow the lawn by simply riding with me on the mower. We buckle up and I put their hands on the steering wheel and let them steer with me together. They also feed the dog, clean the windows with mama, and bring dirty dishes to the counter. There are plenty of ways that children can help out. When they're younger, it will usually be more of a hassle than a help. But remember, you are instilling in them habit of being useful and helping in the family. You are also silently communicating to each of them that they are needed.

Be creative! Realize that although it will be *more* work at first, especially with younger kids, it will be well worth it later on. They will learn that they are needed in their families and in the world in which they live. Children have an innate desire to be needed. But this desire may go dormant if we allow it. God created each one of us for a purpose, so we want to be aware that this purpose is in some way being fulfilled.

Your children's confidence will be high if they have the opportunity to contribute to the family. In America, our affluent lifestyles can be a stumbling-block to letting our children share in the responsibilities. It's much easier to just do it ourselves, or hire someone else to do it. I challenge you, live in such a way that your children are legitimately *needed*.

Do you view your children as producers, not just consumers? Do they view themselves as producers as well? Do they feel that they have something to offer to the family and to the world they live in? This world needs more people who can contribute to needs of humanity. In our free market world, you help people, and in turn you get taken care of too. I believe it was Martin Luther who said, *"God doesn't need your good works, but your neighbor does."* What a powerful thought; with our work, we can love and bless our neighbor.

"The child who is thought of as important, not only in what he does but in what he thinks, is usually well-adjusted. He feels that he is part of the team, that the team wouldn't function quite as well without him. He will begin taking pride in the things he does and he will find ample time to pursue his own development as he begins setting major goals for himself." [19]

—Richard LeFevre 'The Nature of Work'

#23

Answer this question:

Is a child a blank slate and an empty vessel, or is a child a gift to be opened and discovered?

✸

The answer to this question will dramatically affect how we raise and educate our children. In many ways, when we treat a child like a blank slate, we neglect or disregard the gifts that God has placed in them. I submit to you that each child is uniquely gifted by God to be a blessing to the world in a special way. God has created each person for a specific role and purpose in this world, and has gifted them accordingly. Think about your child and their strengths, and their particular calling in life.

Author and educator Chris Davis, in his book *'Gifted'*, explains this best when he says:

"Each child is a unique creation of God, and God has placed within that child very specific giftings and callings. God, then, sends the child into our time-space world to be raised by the adults He has chosen and who are responsible for discovering what God has put within the child. Having begun to discover the child's giftings and callings, parents must then provide the child with the tools and the time to become proficient in those giftings and callings. The purpose is to allow the child to grow up to express what God has put within him or her. This brings glory to God." [20]

—Chris Davis

You've probably heard the expression, "A square peg in a round hole". Maybe you have felt this way about your life or your career. *Could it be that many people feel like they don't 'fit in' because their parents or their society was expecting them to be just like all of the other children?* Schools tend to have a conforming effect on our children and on our culture. Not everyone will be an inventor, but some will. Not all children will be employees, some will be entrepreneurs.

All children have different God-given gifts and interests. Some will be artistic, others will be analytic. *Can you imagine if we were all house builders? Where would our food production be? Or if all were teachers, where would the businessmen be?* Children have different gifts and callings in life. Begin to offer them many diverse experiences to see what they are naturally good at, what they are interested in, and what they enjoy. You will be embarking on an marvelous journey of discovering who God created your little ones to be.

#24

Talk TO and WITH your kids, not just *over* them.

✳

It's easy to get into the habit of talking around or 'over' them, instead of involving them in our conversations. This is challenging, especially with young children. My wife and I often have conversations at the dinner table, and sometimes we realize that we have spent ten minutes talking "over" our kids. Engaged in conversation as if they weren't even there. The kids will then be vying for our attention, each one trying to be louder than the other.

So, instead of just talking over them, why not talk to them, and ask them questions? Asking people questions will show them that you value what they think and what they have to say. Something I have done with my children even before they were talking much was to go over some of the happenings of their day as I was putting them to bed. Bring out the different things that happened throughout the day, and ask them questions, even if they are too young to respond with words. Even babies in the womb benefit from hearing their mothers talk to them. Our children are never too young to be blessed with our words and our attention.

In the past, some well-meaning people had a mindset that children should be seen and not heard. Although I understand the sentiment, I disagree with this view. I do believe children should be respectful and polite, and they can learn these things by having parents purposefully interact with them. That said, there are definitely times where it is appropriate for children to be silent and listen. We seek to train our kids to listen to others and wait for their turn to talk. Sometimes Regina and I have something important to discuss, and we will then instruct our kids to be quiet and let mama and daddy talk. During visiting with others, we also expect our children to be respectful and not interrupt others when they are talking.

A while ago, during a busy and exciting time in our lives, I was driving somewhere with my two-and-a-half year-old daughter, and I began talking to her. She didn't immediately recognize that I was talking to her specifically, because I was asking her questions. Eventually she realized I was actually asking her a question. This was a reality check for me, as I realized that lately I had been neglecting speaking intentionally TO my children. In our busyness, my wife and I had been spending a lot of time talking over them and not letting them participate in our conversations.

Sometimes, all our kids hear from us are reprimands and admonishments. Let's be sure to talk positively and proactively to them more than we have to rebuke or correct them. As we take more opportunities to talk TO them and interact with them, our children will likely open up and want to share more with us. They will share their hopes and dreams with us. We can then help them own their own goals, and plan together with them how to accomplish said goals.

A few years ago, I was on a drive with a friend and his young son. The boy, maybe 2 or 3 at the time, was sitting in his carseat in the backseat. At one point, my friend paused in the midst of our conversation, and looked back to his son. He was trying to say something to his daddy, and my friend intentionally gave him a listening ear. This was something he practiced with his son regularly. Years later, although he is still a "young" boy, he is easily able to interact with adults in a polite and conversational way. My friend's intentionality paid off; his son is well-adjusted and on his way to becoming a young man.

#25

Incorporate your children into your life. Do life together as much as possible. Don't allow your children to become a hindrance to you enjoying life.

✳

In many ways "life" is considered over once children enter the picture; *why is that?* In times past, children were considered vital to the family, and in some cultures, they still are. In these sort of cultures, you will see that the families will often have more children, and the children will generally take part in whatever the family does, whether work or pleasure.

'Do life' together with them as much as possible. Life is a journey, take them along for the ride. For example, we take our three toddlers to formal restaurants, even if some might consider it a non-family friendly place. My wife and I especially like to interact with other *families*, as opposed to just having "guys-night" and "ladies-night".

Let *fellowship* be the focus of your home and family life. Read to them, even out of the books you are reading personally. Have quiet time and read "together" with them. Take them on mission trips with you. Prior to having children in our home, my wife and I have lived overseas and done missions in several different countries. Recently, we took our 3 children on a month-long mission-trip to Africa. *Was it hard?* Yes, it had its challenges, but it was also a very rich bonding experience for all of us as a family.

Involving our children in our lives is becoming increasingly difficult in the post-industrial age. We are often so disconnected as families these days. Fathers, you have huge potential to impact your children by working together with them. I encourage you to let your sons be with you in your work as much as possible (if it is permitted and appropriate). I know of some fathers who cannot involve their children in their work, but they have a 'side-hustle' at home where the children can be involved. Remember, our sons are men-in-training. *If we don't take the time to teach them to be proper men, who will?*

Think about it; we all have secret desires for our children. We may hope that they will be entrepreneurial, or that they will travel adventurously, or that our sons will be outdoorsmen, or that our children will be 'missional'. If we are inwardly desiring our kids to one day live this sort of life, why not do it now? Why not live like that now, so that it won't be unnatural for them to live like that later? Give your kids a vision for living a life that is bigger than themselves.

#26

Talk through problems and issues with your kids.

✳

Take time to talk through the problems and issues that inevitably come up, rather than "sweeping them under the rug" as quickly as you can. Sometimes our tendency can be merely to modify a child's behavior quickly. Behavior-modification alone may avert the situation at hand, but it will probably not solve the underlying issue.

Do our children understand what is going on? Do they understand the issue and why their misbehavior is wrong? We can help them realize not only *what* they did wrong, but *why* it was not appropriate behavior. Yes, this takes more time, but trust me, it will save us time in the long run.

Do we even understand what is going on? If we talk through the problems when they arise, we too can begin to see and comprehend why our children are doing what they are doing. We will come to better understand what our kids are going through, and help them to be able to reshape their own thinking.

Ask yourself, *"What is this child thinking?"* You have probably wondered about that very thing many times, but are we really wondering what the child is thinking, or are we just saying that? We often act out of emotion or feeling, especially when we are young and immature. And our emotions are profoundly impacted and guided by our thoughts. A pastor recently shared this insight with us in a parenting class:

"Feelings, in the emotional sense, largely come from thoughts—consequently, when we have negative and bad feelings, it is very often because we are thinking wrong. So, by learning to think right, we can give considerable direction to our feelings."

—David Wiebe

The truth in the previous statement has been very eye-opening for me in my personal life and in my role as a parent. When a child is scared, or angry, or experiencing adverse emotions, maybe we should ask the questions, "What are they thinking and what thoughts led them to these emotions?" Dealing with bad and improper thinking will in many ways take care of the 'negative' feelings. Also, we do not want to shut our children down emotionally. We want them to learn to express their emotions in an honorable, dignifying, and gentle way.

#27

Show lots of affection as a family.

✳

Mom and Dad, do your kids know that you love each other? They won't be very convinced of your love for them if you don't love each other in an obvious way. Do they see Dad giving Mom a hug or kiss? Do they see Mom rub Dad's shoulders? Or Dad touch Mom lovingly when he walks by her? Do you hold hands? Do you say "I love you" to each other often?

Parents, we develop and determine to a large degree the culture that exists inside our homes. What sort of climate are we producing in our families? Is it a dark and cold one? Or are the fires of love burning warmly in our hearts and homes? My wife and I have created some traditions in our home that help us show more affection. One such tradition is always holding hands whenever we pray together as a family. Sometimes we will have a group-hug after we have devotions or a meal together. Back when I worked away from home, I would always give my wife and each child a hug and kiss before I left for work.

A pat on the back or a hand on the shoulder can speak volumes of affirmation to a child. I will often hold my little one's hand while we are talking together. Affection can be shown in many different ways. One way in which I communicate my affection to my children is that I have made up a song for each of them. This might sound silly, but you can tell that the children hearing me singing their song brings them joy and affirms my love for them. I have also given them some different endearing nicknames that I use frequently. Some parents may have a special greeting or handshake that they use with their kids.

The blessings of showing affection freely in your family are manifold. First off, the recipient of your affection will feel loved. Second, when you are more affectionate to someone, you begin to love them more. Also, when affection abounds between mom and dad and the kids, the kids will become more affectionate with each other as well. Fondness and tenderness will be more natural for your children. That's a win-win!

We often wait until something tragic happens to say the words, *"I love you"*. Why not be real and honest and communicate that love to each other now? Let those walls down and love on each other! That's what family is for!

#28

Practice being unplugged as a family.

�֍

We are living in the digital era. It's interesting how we, as parents, are generally more concerned about our *kids* and *their* use of electronics, not so much about ourselves and our use of electronics and media; this is for good reasons no doubt, but how about us? How are we, the parents, doing in regards to our *plugged-in life*? Are we physically present but mentally absent?

I urge you, stay disconnected from technology as much as possible when you are together with your children. Have set-aside times for emailing, social media, phone calls, etc. We are more *"plugged-in"* to media and electronics than ever today; yet we are more *unplugged* from real life than ever. Our digital addiction stands as an obstacle to fellowship and intimacy in our families. Not only should our children be limited in their use of electronics, but we too should take time to be unplugged. Parents, our children need us to be *present*. I know the temptations and the challenges we face are real. Many of us work and practically live online these days.

According to *Nielsen's Total Audience Report*, Americans aged 18 and older spend more than 11 hours a day on their electronic devices.[21] If you figure in 8 hours of sleep, you're only left with 4-5 hours of time to get ready for the day, eat, spend time with God, fellowship with others, and pour into your kids. And if you factor in how dull and distracted we are when we are using our devices, you know that we are not multitasking well. We are not parenting well when we are constantly on our devices. It is basically telling our children that *this* device, and what it has to offer me, is more important than they are.

We will need understanding and discernment here. It's true that we can learn through our devices, connect with others, get work done, etc. But on the other hand, we can very well be neglecting our kids in the process. Wisdom and understanding is required on our behalf to determine at what point our devices become our *vices*.

Set a certain time that is purely for your family, and 'unplug' during that time. People can call twice if it is an emergency. Be *present*, physically and mentally, with your family. Be attentive and observant and give your people your full attention. The time that we have with our kiddos is short. Let's make it count!

Wherever you are, be all there! Live to the hilt every situation you believe to be the will of God.

—Jim Elliot

#29

Be a YES parent!

✹

What do I mean with this? Am I saying that we should say yes to a child's every request? No, I am not saying that at all, but think about this: most children hear the word *"no"* more than any other word. In fact, according to studies, the average toddler hears the word no *hundreds of times a day!* [22] Now don't get me wrong here, I understand that children *must* be taught what the word 'no' means. And yes, you are right, they cannot have *everything* they want. They must be told "no" at certain times, and we cannot avoid that.

Still, I urge you to be a *yes* parent. As much as possible, say yes as much or more than you say no. This can be done in different ways. First and foremost, when a child says, "Daddy, can we go play catch?", do we think before we say, "No?" Yes, we are tired, but are we *that* tired? Or how about, "Can I help you Mama?" Mama is thinking about how much quicker she can get it done without the little one's help, but what would be more impactful for the child? It's easy to say no; let's think before we drop that two-letter word too quickly.

Let's say your son asks you if he can have a sleepover at a friend's house, and you are not comfortable with that idea. You could just simply say, *"No"*, and leave it at that. Or, you could say, *"No son, you can't do that tonight. But, how about you and I have a camp-out in our backyard instead?"* No to the sleepover, YES to a dad-and-son campout! Let's find and make opportunities to say yes to our children.

With three children of my own, I have had my fair share of experience with toddlers. There are so many moments that call for correction. So many chances to say no come up. It doesn't seem like we have to look for those opportunities. But, what if we started looking for more opportunities to compliment our children on a job well done, to praise them for something done right and applaud their efforts? What if we would appreciate the aspects of their character that are good and noble, and acknowledge their growth and advancement? Praise for what is done right tends to produce more right actions. In fact, studies show that praising and acknowledging good in someone is more effective at producing a positive outcome in someone than condemning and criticizing the bad.

#30

Memorize Scripture and songs together as a family.

✳

One way we memorize Scripture is to go through the ABCs, as a whole family, choosing a Scripture verse for each letter. This is a fun exercise that teaches them about our language and also builds their Scripture repertoire at the same time. Think about it, if the Bible is suddenly made illegal, how much Scripture will we have hidden in our hearts? How much of the Bible do we have committed to memory? Let's give our children that gift!

We have a tendency to be music-addicts in our home. We have grown accustomed to having (good) music playing almost constantly. So, we decide to give Pandora a break sometimes and sing songs in the vehicle together instead of always having the stereo on. When you are sitting around the table, what songs can you sing from memory? Or if you are sitting at the campfire, or in the vehicle, or on a walk? Singing with others knits the hearts together in a special way.

Don't limit your family to just children's songs. Go ahead and work on some lengthier, deep, theology-rich hymns. You may be surprised when your youngsters begin to prefer age-old hymns over your typical children's songs. Songs that are verses of Scripture put to music are great ways to memorize Scripture too.

#31 (BONUS!)

Have fun! Make it a rule to let joy rule in your home.

✳

Parents, in a few short years, our children will be adults, and they will likely move on to start their own families. Time flies! Make a life *together*. A life that is worth living.

Whatever you do, be sure to enjoy your family life! Let joy be a rule in your home and let joy rule in it. A rule we have in our home is that when it comes to play, if it is not fun for everyone involved, don't do it. Sure, it may be fun for brothers to bounce sister around on the trampoline, but if she is not enjoying it, we need to stop. In the same way, if your family is not experiencing joy together, let's find out why. Then, let's take responsibility for whatever is not right or best and make changes for the better.

Take time for each other. Live, laugh, and love. You only have one family, make it a good one!

EPILOGUE:

Being People of *Action*

✳

After reading a book like this, the question that remains is, *"What are you going to do now?"* This book, by its very title and nature, demands action. If there is such a thing as 'intentional parenting', it simultaneously means that there is also such a thing as *'unintentional* parenting'. *Are you going to choose to parent on purpose or not?* Regardless of what you do or do not do, I hope and desire that you recognize the tremendous opportunity you have in raising the children that God has entrusted to you. And whatever you decide to do, think about it, and make an educated, intentional *choice.* Don't abdicate the responsibility of your family's success, well-being, and future to anyone else.

Parents, if your family is the ship, then you are the captains. You are at the helm. Imagine that your children are like the new world in Columbus's day—there is so much to discover! There is an entire new world of possibilities out there! *Your children are* **unique;** *there has never been a person alive who is exactly like who your child is.* Who knows what gifts reside in your children? There is no telling how many blessings will come to the world around you through your children. We need to chart our course intentionally and deliberately, and then set sail!!

One who drifts aimlessly on the seas of life will probably not get to a destination intact. Instead, it is likely that the drifter's ship will be dashed to pieces on the rocky shoreline of shattered dreams. Take care to steer the ship in the direction it should go. A builder that is constructing a house does not simply throw some random materials together to see what will happen. Careful planning goes into every detail and every step is followed. In the same way, you are shaping and building a home and a family. You are raising the next generation to take on the world!

My hope and desire is that you have been inspired to think intentionally about your family life, and that you plan ahead and set your own course. If you get nothing else from this book, but a desire to be more intentional with your family life, I believe this book will have fulfilled its purpose.

Maybe you will start planning with more direction and purpose.

May you leave the reading of this book with a renewed passion to parent with a purpose and to raise your children intentionally. Think about it, you are leading and managing *the most important place on earth*; your home. Take action! Chart a course and steer the ship accordingly; don't just let the waves and wind toss you wherever they please. Don't be a content consumer only, but be a producer, a doer, a person of *action*.

Parents, the investment you make into your children matters in eternity. It is an *eternal* investment. Don't settle for ordinary or what the culture around you considers normal. Pursue *God's* design and vision for your family. He created us, and He has great plans for us. Then, by His grace, go on as a family to live the exceptional life that He has called you to.

In conclusion, I salute you fathers, men at the helm, and your co-captains, mothers, world-changers. Know that I am cheering you on!

ACKNOWLEDGMENTS

First of all, I need to thank my wife, Regina. Thank you for all the encouragement, inspiration, and believing in me. Thank you for all the priceless input and intuition you provided for this project. It would not have been possible without you. I also need to thank John and Helena Harms, for their input and help with the project. Mom and Dad, thank you for parenting me on purpose. Jake Peters, you are a blessing and an inspiration to me. Thank you for all the input and encouragement. Chris Davis, your wisdom and insight is above and beyond. You have helped shape my vision for parenting and education in powerful way.

Also, my children, Benaiah, Abishai, and Zibiah. You guys have shaped me in so many ways in the short time we have known each other. You are my inspiration, and the fire in my bones. And I thank God, who has not only given me this opportunity, but also has given me life.

I have been inspired by a great number who have gone on before me. By many fathers that have led their families well, and mothers that have sacrificed so much to bring up future generations. May God bless you all!

About TutorDad

TutorDad Press was founded out of a passion for intentional parenting. We see parenting as the most important job in the world. So much in this world depends on parents leading their families well. We want to help people parent on purpose. It's an obvious fact that parents are the greatest influencing factor in a child's life. Therefore, parents have the greatest potential to make a lasting impact on the next generation. Parents have the exciting privilege of doing life together with their children and discovering who God created them to be. We believe that parents are experts when it comes to their children. But we all need encouragement and inspiration in our calling as parents. That is what TutorDad is all about. Helping you parent on purpose.

Even before becoming a father, I had a passion for education, especially the education of children. Education is an important part of every life story. I believe that a child's education should equip them for *life*. Education should concern itself with discovering each child's unique gifts, talents, abilities. It should also aim to help each child get closer to finding their passions and calling in life. I have a vision for children leaving the home adequately prepared to take on life vigorously and confidently and live it to the fullest.

Parents have the opportunity to properly equip their children for success. We believe that every parent can be involved in their children's education. You don't need to leave education solely to the 'experts'. You *are* an expert when it comes to your children. Together, we can live, learn, and grow along *with* our children. So why not band together and learn from each other as we are on this exhilarating journey? That's our aim with *TutorDad*. I myself am a parent that is deep in the process of learning how to do this father thing right. Join me as we delve into how to make the best investments we can into the lives of our children.

For more resources, visit our website at:

https://tutordad.org

More parenting on purpose resources can be found here:

https://tutordad.org/resourcesforparenting

We Love Feedback!

How do you parent on purpose? What have you learned in the course of your parenting career? I would absolutely love to hear more ideas from you. Also, if this book has encouraged you, I would be thrilled to hear about it!

Send your feedback to:
johnathan@tutordad.org

If this book inspired and encouraged you, I'd greatly appreciate a review on Amazon. :-)

#parentingonpurpose
#tutordad
#raisingthefuture
#intentionalparenting
#childrenareablessing

CITATIONS:

1. Robert Wolgemuth *'The Most Important Place On Earth'* (W Publishing Group and Imprint of Thomas Nelson, 2004, 2016)
2. Chris Davis, *'Gifted: Raising Children Intentionally' (Pioneer Homeschooler Publications, 2014)*
3. Jim Rohn, *https://www.goodreads.com/author/quotes/657773.Jim_Rohn, (9-7-18)*
4. Glenn Doman and Janet Doman, *'How To Teach Your Baby To Read' (Square One Publishers, 2006)*
5. Masterfoods: *https://www.popsugar.com/moms/Kids-Say-Whom-World-Want-Invite-Dinner-40282816*
6. Stephen R. Covey *'The 7 Habits of Highly Successful People' (Simon & Schuster 1989, 2004)*

7. Jim Rohn, *https://www.brainyquote.com/quotes/jim_rohn_3855 14 (9-7-18)*

8. *https://www.brainyquote.com/quotes/johann_wolfgan g_von_goeth_121252 (9-7-18)*

9. Darren Hardy, *'The Compound Effect' (Vanguard Press, SUCCESS Media 2010)*

10. Josh McDowell, *'Straight Talk With Your Kids About Sex' (Josh McDowell Ministries 2012 Harvest House Publishing)*

11. Darkness To Light *https://www.d2l.org/the-issue/statistics/*

12. "Dream-poster" as found in Chris Davis', *'Gifted: Raising Children Intentionally'*

13. Adapted from Merriam Webster and Thesaurus.com https://www.thesaurus.com/browse/tradition?s=t

14. H. Clay Trumbull *'Hints On Child Training' (Great Expectations Book Co.)*

15. Jacqueline Kennedy Onassis: *https://www.brainyquote.com/quotes/jackie_kennedy_ 127001 (9-7-18)*

16. George R.R. Martin: *https://www.goodreads.com/quotes/408441-a-reader-l ives-a-thousand-lives-before-he-dies-said (9-7-18)*

17. Edith Schaeffer, *'What Is A Family?' found on website:*

*https://fiveinarow.com/blog/2013/02/13/youre-the-cur
ator-of-your-familys-museum/*

18. Gary Chapman and Ross Campbell *'The 5 Love
    Languages of Children: The Secret to Loving
    Children Effectively' (Northfield Publishing 1997,
    2005, 2012)*

19. Richard LeFevre, 'The Nature of Work', as found
    in *'A Bluestocking Guide Economics' by Jane A.
    Williams, Bluestocking Press 2015)*

20. Chris Davis, *'Gifted: Raising Children
    Intentionally'*

21. https://www.nielsen.com/content/dam/corporate/
    us/en/reports-downloads/2018-reports/q1-2018-to
    tal-audience-report.pdf

22. https://sueatkinsparentingcoach.com/2017/01/231
    37-2/

✵ NOTES & IDEAS

✴ NOTES & IDEAS

✸ NOTES & IDEAS

✸ NOTES & IDEAS

✳ NOTES & IDEAS

✴ NOTES & IDEAS

✵ NOTES & IDEAS

✺ NOTES & IDEAS

✳ NOTES & IDEAS

✸ NOTES & IDEAS

✴ NOTES & IDEAS

✳ NOTES & IDEAS

✸ NOTES & IDEAS

www.ingramcontent.com/pod-product-compliance
Lightning Source LLC
LaVergne TN
LVHW051414080426
835508LV00022B/3080